SELECTED POEMS

Celtic Blood

Selected Poems
1968   1994

Philip Daughtry

New Native Press
1995

Some of the poems in this volume have first appeared in the following magazines, anthologies, periodicals, and journals: *Western Poetry Review, Greenfield Review, Co-Evolution Quarterly, Colorado State Review, Beatitude, Ecology Newsletter, NEW Canadian & American Poetry, Big Moon, City of Buds and Flowers, Kyoi-Kuksu, Wood Ibis, Kuksu, Katuah Journal, Whole Earth Catalog #34, Mendocino Grapevine, Western Slopes Connection, Pinch Penny, Empty Bowl, Blind Donkey, Coyote's Journal, Snowy Egret.*

Poems from *The Stray Moon* and *Kid Nigredo* were published in limited letterset bound editions by Turkey Press.

"Nuclear Waste" was published as a fine-editions broadside in 1979 by New Native Press.

"Big Wombhearted Man" first appeared as a broadside published by Dale Pendell and Exiled In America Press.

"Doon Pit" was published in 1977 as a broadside by Sombre Reptiles Press.

ACKNOWLEDGEMENTS
I would like to thank Thomas Crowe for his longtime support and dedication to lyric poetry; Galway Kinnell for his teaching; Jerry Ratch and Terry Marquez both for their good humor and honest camaraderie; Dave Philips for his kinship; Steve Kiralla, Bruce Mulloy and Steven Kirsch for their loyalty to our men's group over the last five years; Dale Pendell for his relentless insight; Steve Peck for his friendship in our collaborative filmic writing; Huguette Patenaude for her spirited support, Gioia Timpanelli for her conversation; Califia Suntree—who made the trip to North Carolina through tornadoes and a tropical rainstorm; Nan Watkins for her eagle-eye proofreading patience; and Salley for her inspiration. I am also appreciative of Gary Snyder whose cheerful zen and ethno-poetic urged me into the bones of my own Geordie origins. My decision to persevere and trace the faint, salty poet's road in the face of general resistance was initiated by Robert Bly in 1968—a man whose influence I am indebted to, both through his translations, poetry, and courage in our generative American labor toward initiating the mature masculine.
—Philip Daughtry

Cover photo by Mark Olencki, 1994

Book design by Dana Irwin, Irwin Graphics, Asheville, N.C.

New Native books and broadsides are published for Thomas Rain Crowe and New Native Press. Inquiries and book orders should be addressed to: New Native Press, P.O. Box 661, Cullowhee, N.C. 28723.

Library of Congress Catalog Card #94-69076

ISBN 1-883197-05-8

This book is for
my daughter Califia and my son Sean

"Look! Here's a bargain;

give one life, and take a hundred!"
(Rumi)

CONTENTS

PREFACE

With all the ancient requisites of a Celtic bard ("of lowly birth, on a high place, and by running water"), Philip James Daughtry was born during an air raid in the Manor House of the Earl of Derwentwater just outside of Newcastle in Northumberland on the north-east coast of England in 1942. The male half of a set of twins, he was born a Geordie only a stone's throw from the River Tyne. But aside from his link to the coal mines of Newcastle, Philip Daughtry also had a strong link to the Americas as evidenced in his middle name, "James." His grandmother was Thomasina James, who was a relative of the legendary outlaw brother team of Frank and Jesse James.

In 1957, Daughtry emigrated to a Cree Indian Reservation in Canada before moving to New York City in 1961. Looking very much like a young Frank James, as an expatriot Geordie bard he began his poetic journey as well as his dream of living out events portrayed in stories and films he had heard and seen as a boy in England, of the "Wild West."

I have followed the work of Philip Daughtry (alias Suntree) for almost twenty years. During this time I have seen him, like a coyote or a chameleon, change his voice/colors from urban outlaw, to backcountry eco-activist, to Gaelic bard, to Hollywood screenwriter, to cowboy poet. In this collection of *Selected Poems*, Geordie-born poet Philip James Daughtry stands up in the attire of immigrant incarnations as manifest in representational book manuscripts (published and unpublished) from over a 30-year history. From the late '50s and his immigration to the U.S. from northern England (**Early Poems**); to the '70s and his double life in San Francisco and Berkeley *(Stray Moon)*; to the '80s and his association with the *Kuksu* poets who'd gathered in a community that included Dale Pendell, Gary Snyder, and the ghost of Lew Welch in the

Sierra Foothills *(Kid Nigredo, Celtic Blood)*; to the '90s and his life in Hollywood and Los Angeles *(Crouching Over The Kill)*, Daughtry has gone the long way 'round to have finally arrived, with *Selected Poems*, at home with his expatriot American voice.

The interiors of these poems range from purely bardic influences as evidenced most profoundly in the section *Celtic Blood* housing his Geordie poems (and in this, Daughtry may be the only poet in North America writing in this dialect), to lyrically narrative poems such as "Eclipse" from later poems included in *Crouching Over The Kill*. In all cases, the poems are persuasively and percussively lyric. His (heart) beat is to a "canny old drum"—an indigenous water drum, filled with "Celtic blood." And in this sense, Philip Daughtry may be the best synthesis of ancient Celt and purely modern American writing in English today. Wafting between his early roots as mirrored in the work of fellow Northumberian Basil Bunting and Welsh bard Bobi Jones, to that of his American mentors James Merrill, Galway Kinnell and the Beats, Daughtry emerges with an emotional honesty which, when coupled with his unquestionable craft, punctuates the strong spiritual quality of these poems.

Truly a soul split between past and present, in terms of heritage; Britain and the Americas, in terms of allegiance to place; and the traditional vs. the modern, with regard to literary time—Philip James Daughtry has, in his poetics and in his verse, conquered that schizophrenic split and has created a collaborative "other" which is, at once, oral and written-to-be-read. No small feat, this, and this and his celebratory vision of cultural diversity and planetary harmony are reasons enough for the publication, the purchase, and the reading of this book.

Thomas Rain Crowe
September, 1994

I.

EARLY POEMS

(1968 - 1973)

· ❦ ·

MUSE

Certainly
      she is more alive than dead
   Her body
      scattered upon more leaves than beds
   permitting me
to wind this sensual curiosity on limbs
      where now I am more truly hung.

THERE IS NO PLACE
THAT IS NOT LOOKING
(after Rilke)

This urge to sing alone on the street at night
walking past store windows
where the haunted fashions wait,
lowering my voice for police,
raising it to reach across to the dead.

Singing because I was nurtured on great movies
and because each day their country
becomes less and less a labor of the heart.

First, we ground the stone into metal and into cogs
and shred by shred we become torn by paper.
There are men dissolving the nervous system
underground in Utah with invisible gas,

it is because we killed the buffalo by millions
that we know how a species can vanish.
It is because the modern ear beats a path to the mind
where sparks of peace drown in a sea of reason,

I am alone on this street. I have been alone: singing
on the streets of Leningrad, Helsinki, Mexico City,
New York, Los Angeles, the muse chill
thrown along my back like Odin's dice,

knowing this is where I belong, wanting America
like my first girl, on the shore of a world
promised by my fathers
who stooped out of dark mines
reaching with trembling hands for tickets to a new life.

BRAZIL '68

(Gracias al Union Carbide Chemical Co.)

In the summer heat with women and children
we marched twenty miles,
twenty miles to these pipes fouling the river
and no-one is here. No-one to hear us.

> Padre de Freitas waits in the mountains.
> Our village faces death straight ahead.

In front of the plant our spokesmen
repeat what each of us knows,
but iron and steel hum in the river
while the government does nothing.

> Padre de Freitas waits in the mountains.
> We ask an end to this progress that kills us.

The river is poisoned.
Our river of bread where
fishermen and fish live and die together.
Behold the hour, we demand a solution.

> Padre de Freitas waits in the mountains.
> Only a fugitive to lead us, not help us.

The people of Carvelhos
must have clear water
flowing in the river,
for we rot in a village
dying of hunger.

> Padre de Freitas waits for the people.
> Quietly we join him to fight in the mountains.

· 🌿 ·

NEVSKY PROSPECT

Esenin, Esenin,
I am here in the light around you
in love again with ice,
the cold flung from your heart
bears clinging to my neck.
Esenin,
your city spits columns,
ballerinas who walk on lakes.
When I steal your books,
the letter *R* smokes,
the village of my childhood
is invaded by salmon, and
I am instantly a poet of people
hustling America
with ears that fly away to sea.
Even my arms
raised all day to miles of paint
discover they are after all
only two hungry birds
and remember Leningrad
as the bow of a frozen ship whose
snowfooted sailors
hunt in the forest
to discover me
undressing that Kazakh,
freezing us with eyes like wolves.

(Leningrad, 1973)

AN OLD SONG

The young girls, the young girls
they hear my voice
and cannot hide how they're afraid.

What is it I must know?
Perhaps my beard,
perhaps the smile of my babies
from the world beneath a sky,

perhaps the unfledged stare of friends
gone ahead into the fiery plunder.
See. Now they are giggling.
Their bodies are giggling.

Perhaps my eyes remember these girls
far away as Cadiz.

The young girls, young girls
how they admire me.
Admiration distant as a great sea rock.

II

THE STRAY MOON

(1975)

· 🌿 ·

Free'd horse

    rambles onto clover

drifts into purple

    kicks the sky!

BIGTIME RIVERMAN
TEMPORARILY FALLS SICK
AND DIES

Maybe
I am lying crosslegged
  too happy in the middle of too many nights.
      Inside me is another man,
        another man inside struggling to find the way
          waiting for me to be bored and wholly drown.
        When I drown, the last bubbles
  were full moons, when I sang
 I sang and the dreams came in the dark.
And this other man is in no hurry
      the same as how I waited
      asking my turn.
And this man after I drown
    will speak like me,
      his memory will include me
      as sand always knows
how we have forgotten the story
where I rest my head telling pain
        to come from underground,
      giving myself to the river,
refusing to make more words
  that carry blood away from the river.

MULCH

The news will be
there is no leaving
no quitting this Earth
only the coming back
the return
speckled on plastic wings
of ladybugs
crawling like venetian blinds
wrinkled on bellies of sowbugs
one day
gathered for new wine
farmers will dance slow circles
maggots curled in their palms
like children.

THE CLOSING UP

Night came with its chains,
moths clung to the windows;
the trees embraced themselves
like ladies at an accident.

Faces were haunted
by the undersides of coins,
limousines of old suits
passed in the darkness.

The children's guns
lay among pictures
of women with blue hair,
walls grew slowly to glass
and each house drew up its eaves
like feet.

RIVA RIDGE

Shuffling feather fresh snow
soot smell of winter
crunched across drift dunes
the *curd curd* of boots
through whitefish scales
across dove wings
star speckled
I take the Earth's rise
Earth lifting
through snow fall and star rush
squinting through snow fields
ghost hulks of trees
my shadow thrown down huge
distances turning
as hands measure fire
I breathe this spirit place
impassive mountains
peripheral light glimmers
mucked under voices
souls shivered on the wind

BAD WATER

Tanks advance through low valley fog,
    treads greased thick with river rats,
tanks seeking longeared owls
    to end their glide from east to west,
all along the San Joaquin tanks come,
    a business sweating under iron skin
creating curses, creating reasons for why
    men dump poison and shoot wild birds
seeing choices weave into maggots
    while owlwings sunglued to blacktop
strain to tear highways from earth and
    tanktreads ladder the ground
where rivers made too slow for fish
    wait under bridges for the guns
illuminating kitchens where women
    fold housewife hands into flowers
fingering their parts in the massacre
    until vastness once given to birds
can no longer bear wings
    and machineries beat out breath
a rhyme for each gesture, each need,
    as farmers grapple for intercourse
humping cannon through low valley fog
    coming to kill the redtail hawk
coming to kill the longeared owl.

WINGBEATS

Old mothers
    old fathers
you gave me this brain
like cold supper
    in poor houses in Italy
      a memory
    like antlers
  stolen from attic cleanouts
and I have filled its space
    with souvenirs,
      shells,
      feathers,
      smoke,
    at night
    I feel the moth
flutter wings onto my back
flying in the darkness
    how could I be afraid?

FIRE IN THE EARTH

I was led to touch

  so many places with my head

      I ran off

became

a gypsy

  thirsty

     to touch pyramids

       with my tongue,

 in Tikal

looking down an old dream

   I threw myself

    at the sun:

   look out woman;

I'll tear a broken heart

   straight

    from your petticoat.

MOON

No hole at the whale's mouth
    widens
        round as you,
    where I fly
in the tunnel of your eye
stars vanish.
Like smoke
    from my mother's breast
      I come to you
and in gliding light
      find a bright shore.

AT WOUNDED KNEE

I wanted to fall
    like a deer at full run.
When they took my ankles
      and trailed me away
      I remembered leaves
        sticking to my tongue.

WOLVES

Shadow slink

in each eye

a wolf vision'd world

leaps from the moon

returning

through broken stars

children

who rub worn antlers

children waking

without a solitary wolf

to sing who they are.

HORSE-MAN

When the colt

flares nostrils at the wind

when his legs

are too long

for this world

when his gallop

is winter

we run further than morning

we run

faster than morning!

WHEN SKY DOGS JUMP

It didn't matter
horse, elephant, or snake

didn't matter
whitewater tumbled

didn't matter
touch

spread seasilt
beds of tentacles

a dream open
its procession *moaning*

didn't matter
skyrust on cirrus mesa

didn't matter
knees on trilobites

sinking
loosed gyre springs

didn't matter
the moons riding

didn't matter
widening deserts

didn't matter
she is come so fully

didn't matter
to our body travelling.

·꧁·

Cold

night

alone

I

lie

face down

waiting

for

someone

to crawl

under my body

and pack

the hollows

of

my bones

with

moist

earth.

FROM THE MOON'S IRIS

In woods alone

     my heart

   was a chanting body

fox

   sang loudest

his skulls

a cemetery of mice

fit thin fingers

    (surely

       I am wed

     to musky dens)

but silence

swept electric air

a claw

   swallowed

   spat me free

dropped beneath an elm

  by *owl*

     the owl who steals

     the men who

        fly.

THIS IS THE POEM OF BONES
(Fort Sill, Oklahoma)

This is the poem of bones:

the splay-feet of the buffalo

cannot tell our song,

lonely as an owl's skull,

lonely as caves of teeth in the grass.

This is the poem of bones:

in the camps of the trees

deerflies are lost,

white elbows of water

have nowhere to go.

This is the poem of bones:

new snow chases a coyote's howl,

light drifts through eyewells

scraping the dust;

the wind hunts everywhere for us.

DRIFTING WEST IN THE PACIFIC

for C. Doctorow

I have been away
in a blue light,
my body cast off,
butting its way south
to heaven like a whale.

Along a cobbled shore
I climb ledges,
uprooted small trees
to lean on my eyes
that I might stare
at the unflinching sun.

My toes crimp the sand;
I feel my tongue
slur back with the wind,
my sloth-like hands
trail in the sea.

I am visible as a hair
pricked from the skin;
soon, I will lie
in the piebald earth,
the rise and fall of the hills
my only breath.

III.

KID NIGREDO

(1978)

· ❧ ·

Take me deep to love the dark
 tend my forge
   bend my silver horseshoes
  so I may rise to greet the Sun
    and gain its shining body.

KID NIGREDO

I am this kid of a darkness
suckled on light

as light at evening
slips from the western rim
what is within slips also without

no difference!

Like a shawl in rough hands
my solitude clings
opening the space that is last to die.

CAPTURING AMERICAN HISTORY

After too long
sons and daughters
begin to squint at the Sun.

That night fate shakes Her bones
the kid from nowhere wins a song contest
his mother qualifies
for aid to a moon of her choice.

All across country
dark horses appear on a field of light.

The old guard hunch at the table
cards up their sleeves slip to the floor
crows fly away chuckling *LOOK OUT LOOK OUT.*

· 🌿 ·

GOBIERNO

Men without hope came riding
machetes, pistolas, reatas,
saddles snaked in gold and silver
each one of them surrounded us
in the shadow of his sombrero
and because they did not know
what they wanted, each door is torn open.
The eldest of our village
a man of whitest hair
the blind milk of his eye,
his shirt had been to the river
on the stones of seven sisters,
his life was so white
it made men squint.
A blade made a space
between his head and our body,
   ONLY DUST, DUST AND BLOOD the men said;
not one of them knew
who might have been their father
and when they have counted
everything we hoard for our lives
they whip their horses,
but every year they return
until our village has become theirs :
                         desperados.

HARMONICAS

A voice crouches over a heart
handed to it
by a friend
listening
in the salty places married men go
to seek in ordinary cloth
a secret weave of things.
The voice floats over its life
like flamingos
wavering home over dark sands
and every part of the man
surrenders
because he has reached an age
to smell death
and in its sexual solitude
wonders what to do
with the loneliness of desire
when night slides clouds
between darkness and a slipping moon
casting from our bones
these masculine shadows
as we play our rambling music
from flaw to flaw
herding jumped-up exclamations
to a close
made easy by the journey in us
whose destinations are these midnight
gatherings of clan.

THE EMBARCADERO AT NIGHT
(San Francisco, 1977)

The loneliness of farewells
still waits between the heave and the night tide
and enormous buildings of the wharf
here and there in little knots
a few immigrants who died long ago sit waiting
and although their gaze rises and drops with the waters
and their eyes have become the eyelets in steel cable
they whisper in the same spinal shudders
comforted only by immense distance of the stars.
I have seen gulls wheel among last farewells,
farewells as deep as countries, grandfathers, grandmothers;
watched languages tossed from the stern of ships
moaning with the weight of what they must bear away.
When someone so loved steps across the water to leave
the instant of knowing they will never return
seizes us in a fierce shadow without arms
and inside the ordinary size of a hollowed day
we find our soul in a body like a ring lost in a well.
Still the tide swells and retreats with so many voices
that I return in the evening to listen
and drift with the heart of the sea as it comes
knowing voices return to the same destination
and the cleansing of everything I have created as life
dances in the waves as they are lit by the moon
a desire with time for its song and Earth for its flesh
an offering so tender that here on the Embarcadero
small gatherings of ghosts walk through me without haste
delivering me from sorrow to this audience of air.

MARCH

It begins to rain late at night.
    Wind, like someone breathing into a fire.

I think the wind has come so late
to speak alone with the trees.

I look through my town to see
people asleep in beds.
    In platforms built by the Crow for their dead.

Now the wind enters my small room.
    Trembling dust off the peacock feather.
    I remember to go wherever it wants me.

CONCHO

Reach inside

can't fly another step

find nothing

where my self runs out

pray so hard

hands hurt

dark

in this body

where the work begins.

DIANA

What will unleash her, fiery

walking as willow whips

ten thousand green tongues,

when will the furl of her sashay

lick at my calves

and a moon through an oak

shatter night's shade

casting huge antlers on the moon.

DUSK

Picked her out by curiosity

miles ago

made some promises

kept the night she removed

those clouds

the effulgent foil of undress

tumbling so far

her ancient labor spoke

of course her breast

of course her thigh

of course our lives unspoken

there in the bedroom

at the bottom of the world

we made our dance

and what changed hands

pricelessly the doors swing wide

a moon sits starkly sorrowful

to miss the hesitation of our kiss.

OIL

The wife lies

on her back

lives open

to their nightly drilling

after years

she is a land

gashed, denuded

of trees, birds, fish,

her husband

sees her surface veins

bleat silence

a life

he measures in barrels

as in greased silence

he slaves

hypnotized

by their own blood pumping

pumping

pumping.

RUBBING VELVET

On clear nights, running against the dark

muttering crazy music

a carpet of pine needles for wings

feet don't leave the ground

my eyes swallow darkness whole

the instant

I scare up a thought

an ankle catches a stump

the body skids down a clay bank

on hands and knees

wrestling a manzanita thicket

trailing circles round myself

the deer don't give a damn

flicking their ears

standing stifflegged in the leaves.

HAYING

Shattering looseness of light in hay

musk of the new moon

a pitchfork pierces

tish tish

tines slip sunburnt iron

the squat stack settles

burrheaded sheaves

legs brace on stubble

eaves for the rick

wrestled, whu-ay

hup hup a whattizzz

skypulse, hayquill jab

jab—here's your mind

see our unweaving frayed basket

bones and summer thunder

wing of these arms harvesting

ON THE DENVER & RIO GRANDE

Our holy slow train flashes silverblue
  lapis lazuli on flat brown land
a lady in high velvet knows
  what precious stone to hide
so much hidden by trinkety love
  shades a witch where an angel stands

at whistle stops I offer all my teeth
  a coyote smile of absolute belief
pale sleepless swans her lifted hands
  "lapis lazuli does no harm," she smiled
our holy slow train takes its arc
  stretching West our fantasy for miles

mountains bared their shoulder to the Sun
  the light surrounded us with glass
(our dance belongs in bright museums)
  a voice demanded *tickets into town!*
Colorado, you and me awakened slow
  stepping from a silver train to snow.

HANDCUFFS

You understand, I'm slow

it was just a touch

cops in leather coats

stylish revolvers

and then those fancy bracelets

metal getting warm on wrists

years sleeting by the window

dust of the solitude

crowded with loneliness

poems

with stripes on their arrival

a few joints

cops and robbers

bulletholes in the backseat

my body has been worn outside before

quick as silk pajamas

I write anywhere, die anywhere.

TO LIVE BY THE SEA

Some days collapsing

heavy enough

to throw bones on the ground

I drift with the man

who threw himself

from the tallest building

up there he could see

Earth has a crust

he longed to break through

the crowd

wanted him to fall

from the highest place

JUMP they said

JUMP THROUGH THE CEMENT

and when he came down

broken as a gallon of wine

people ran

to see his fists closing

and from their hands

I am falling

falling

miles through the salty grass.

DEADWATER

Earth commands life

our moonrise

razors between labor

to slit dark eyes

where earth lies dreaming

waters smoke

along air's dreamroads

algae stall

Reactors plumb the darkness

hone a ceaseless lance

piercing each bone.

NUCLEAR WASTE

LOOK FOR ME IN SHADOWS
WHERE GHOSTLY, SPERM FURLS IN THE NIGHT
A CUMULUS OF FISHES
NETS WHERE SCHOLARS
SPLIT ATOMS OF TUMBLING LIGHT
LOOK FOR ME FLYING OVER ROOFTOPS
IN DREAMS OF A THIEF
FINDING NOTHING TO TAKE, NOTHING TO GIVE
LOOK FOR ME THROUGH EYES
OF YOUR FINAL CHILDREN
LOOK FOR ME IN FROZEN SOLITUDE
OF YOUR KITCHEN DOOR
LOOK FOR ME IN THE SHUFFLE
OF A STARVING HORSE
LOOK FOR ME AS YOU LOOK FOR INFINITY
BEFORE EACH SLEEP
LOOK FOR ME BECAUSE FINGERS
RE-APPEAR AT EDGES OF THE KNIFE
LOOK FOR ME IN DISHWATER
SOLIDIFIED TO DREAD
LOOK FOR ME IN VARICOSE RIVERS
SUNK BENEATH YOUR CITY
LOOK FOR ME THROUGH WINDOWS
WHERE THE SKY OPENS ITS OWN MIND,
COGS GRIND IN YOUR SPINE
AND SALAMANDERS WRITHE BENEATH THEM
LOOK FOR ME CLINGING
TO EARTH'S LOST RAFT
LOOK FOR ME ON YOUR OWN STAR
THAT DREAMS TO PIERCE YOUR SKIN
LOOK FOR ME WHEN JUDGES REMOVE BLACK ROBES
LOOK FOR ME IN YOUR BONES
SEARCH THEM, DISCOVER THEIR WINGS,
LUMINOUS BEDS UNDER FALLEN TREES
WHERE SMALL GRUBS BREATHE,
EXPLORE THE GALAXY THAT IS YOUR BODY
BECAUSE DEATH HAS POWER OF AIR
MEN STEAL DARKNESS
SPEAK LIES ABOUT THE MOON
AND LIKE GOLD, THE EARTH'S FLESH BURNS.

IMMIGRANTS
for Murietta

American all the way from England

　　English all the way from Newcastle

　　　Geordie all the way from Ireland

　　　　Irish all the way from Spain!

In Hermosillo, a woman watched

me singing down a dark ride south

a lute beside an oud

our emerging guitar's wildflung song

hands strumming visions

our deep eye's whisper

when history opens wide its arms

and Californians

return to mountains

laughing how they have always known.

IV.

CELTIC BLOOD

(1980 - 1988)

. ❦ .

A poem's a prison

　　bards escape

　　　from a merlin's perch

see birthing and a wake.

THE SWANS OVER KILLINGWORTH

During the war over broken glass, the war over coal
    and bloodsopped bread,
        I was a lamb, a wee Geordie lad of the fields
    who played in bomb craters where cuckoos sing.

My grandfather kept pigeons, calm in his warlock way
    a fate-riddled sergeant
        with a wyrd lads get from too much death.

We walked the marshes and the moors, measuring a day
    by a kestrel's eye
        and kneeling over feathers of Northumberland.

Longnecked, crosses in a faithful brace, swans flying
    pierced me more
        than the village church's splaylimbed God.

If Jesus had white wings, swan mothering eyes, a lake, a nest,
    I'd be no more a Celt;
    praise nails then for all muse waking birds.

BIG WOMBHEARTED MAN

Grandfather was a sergeant in the first War
    and when he stood up in his council kitchen
        he stood up
and from his shoulders bones fell, fell to the floor
    with the gypsy tapdance of bones
and when he spoke
    voices muttered under the North Sea,
        under the garden where potatoes waited
staring from ten thousand eyes, regiments of
                thinskinned potatoes.
And when my grandfather answered, when I asked
    how...he led his lads...over the top?
Bones put on their uniforms of blue winding veins,
    their weaponry of eyes, tongues, wisp white hair
and my grandfather took my hands to say:
        "steady bonnie lambs"
        then we walked, slow men across the fields.

THROUGH THE HERON'S EYE
(Durham 1955)

It was Madame Florrie, a cheap Newcastle "sees all" doing
    fortunes from a knackered cart, that saw my feathers.
Said, I was a kid for the weather of dreams, for hunting nests,
    for watching the way birds fly and the way men
    walk (few, like a Heron measuring rivers, most
grey flannel clerks in a run for the train).

                        I remember
    flowers on her pinny, fingernails—amber, hooked
    to a witch crookedness.
Her cigarette throat arranging fate's transportation:
    "aye, me bonnie lamb, tek heed of the wadin bird,
    depart through its eye."
Gypsy doubletalk, a fingernail SNAP as she turned a card
    slowly in a swallowing way.
                     Later, when Aunt Mary died,
in her dim moan I felt what is by what is not,
    saw how the dying go
flying from widening sockets, out—out on a bus fume'd street.
    And I whisper "Florrie,"
reckoning my past through fields I stride to keep peace
    with an intimate wren
or attempting to collect a brazen Cuckoo who robs its way
    from life to life.
Aye, Florrie, I am at ease in hedges, well away from trams,
    at home in the reality of my desire.
Did I choose its limits, or did you sell me solace
    all for a shilling on the way from school?
                        Older,
with a beardrasp turn on my suspicious pillow, as the moon
    offers milk to the deepchested dark, I imagine
(like Caesar Vallejo who named his death day) going,
going through my clan's iris, meek as a tiger through hoops
    going through the Heron's eye.

LILY

Lily, I was born to be this Geordie poet
with a toothpick in his teeth
to laugh at booze and suicide and literary grief.

My eyes are holes inside the Universe
for songs like laser beams
my bus-stop skeleton rattles when the coldwar touches dreams.

Lily, if I fall asleep inside the middle class
it's all because I let it
kiss my existential ass.

KEEP JUMPING THROUGH
THE FIRE

In May, aye when sunbeams drift
                    their spiderstrings
            to weave because
        into eyes these eyes did fall
me lass and lad
            agree to mumble at this world
                a litany intelligent as Spring
        and say
                I DO.
        It was a month when flowers
                    seize our brains,
            we had an only son
            so bought three rings.
After ceremony,
        home
            where roads are wed
            bread and fiddle faded onto champagne lips
        sworn
                to seasons
truth among oor kitchensmells
                    we share the labor of bold friends.

GANNIN TE MEET THE SUN

Wyfe an yer wimminclan
aa'm a man gannin te meet th Sun

enterin wicca dark
great Moon hoose
wheor clues keep

aa thank ye for widenin eyes
guidin me
te tides that shift me oon odd sea.

Eftor shared an various light
on oor bodies
intimacy maaks distance te see road

knowin ye understand
me, peaceful as marra te aal things.

GOING TO MEET THE SUN

Wife and your womanclan
I am a man going to meet the Sun

when I enter intuitive darkness
that great Moon house
where so many clues reside

I thank you for widening these eyes
and for guiding me
to tides that shift my particular ocean.

After sharing the various light
upon our bodies
intimacy grows a distance to see my road

knowing you understand
how peaceful I am as kin to all things.

DOON PIT

Gannin doon pit
hard-on wi hackin beuts
shullin coals frae National Coal Board
excivatin devil's arsehole tae make rent
wi passin flesh clag on bone
wee sputter on heed tae kna deeth wi
in darks' hoyed-on posh clobber

aye, knaa deep doon in groond thoo song

moons off in dream like faery lamp
suns blueblind milk in pony's eye
gutrot and bogdew o' seam
mebbe noo an daylang ribs iv aad snake
tek shull ti fossil anyroad, hoy'r in tub
spit black lungflowers nowt but pitwheels frae eyes

knaa deep doon in groond thoo song

hand i' dark wierd, hug iv deep doon
cannae tek roof off
sweatdeep blud in pit hackor
ear iv landbreeth, broodfire
grave oppens wi glad hand
breeth's wark aal a dream caul'd leef.

DOWN THE MINE

English translation

Going down the pit
hard at it with hewing boots
shoveling coal for the National Coal Board
excavating the devil's asshole to make the rent
with this passing flesh stuck to bone
a small lamp on your head to recognize death
in darkness' fancy thrown-on clothes

yes, know deep in the ground your song

the moon's off in a dream like a faery lamp
the sun's blueblind milk in a pony's eye
gut-rot and compost dew of the coalface
maybe now and all day the ribs of an old reptile
take shovel to the fossil anyway, throw it in a tub
spit blacklung flowers only pitwheels for eyes

know deep down in the ground your song

hands of the fate that follows you, the deep embrace
where you can't remove the roof
and sweat deep as blood in a coalminer
our ear of the land's breath, brooding fire
the grave opens with a glad hand
breath's work all a dream in life's caul.

CELTIC BLOOD

Milky galaxy of bards who hammer song,
    pale riders in oor Goddess' barn
as eyes grow dark wi wisdom's swoon,
     who teaches men when men lie doon?

Half a god divides us; shame, his darlin food
     sweet moonlight silvers madness
     aye, dare lovers keep night bold
fiercely off theor anvil scud sparks of Celtic gold.

LAY OF A CELT

Aa went te chorch wi Sun days
it was a law
me mates sat in back
an et oor sweets

ye wor hung up nigh deeth lad
wi nails in thoo,

for why i cannae tell.
Noo yars iv come an bloody, gone

girlhearted Jesus
let not men
feed thoo Father anithor country.

NED'S ILLUMINATION
(The Rising Sun/Colliery, 1951)

Ye need
    a lamp in the bliddy dark
      to see the walls of hell
some minty mutton in yer chops,
        dew from a witch's well.
Mind oot for all yer doin
      a canny lamb at work
div'n be ower greedy
    hewin coal like Turks
      excavatin shadows,
        smashin at the dark
      plenty Geordie miners
    larn the night has sparks.
Aye, it's the 'Divil's Arsehole'
    some say, 'Angel's Keep'
        servin time doon here lad
        puts pit lamps in yer sleep.

THE DRAGON SINGER

Bring iz me shapin tool an me dollop
nouts changed
        ah spit ye buggers oot
            al ye buggers

it's the clamour o me Da's teeth
he sleeps on the cooch in Seghill Pit
eftor meetin wi Dragon an gettin wed

        it's mold on me noo
me bad back
an the Sight from hogs iv wierd scrumpy

        More Beer!
            (Ah'l petrify the bliddy town in a minit!)

Ah see yiz
  struttin in yer liberated jodhpurs
                small nekkid pups
                    runnin aboot wi goat's balls
                wankin on the pigheaps
            scroungin a life wi a snake's eye
warm in yer nitpecked sleep
plannin higher walls, wider moats
            fingerin yer daze
        shiversharp dragonword tucked away
grateful ye divn't hae tae offer me the odd sheep

BAAAAAA! Am back.
When ah slithered oot of Jarrow Slats
  aye, ye knew this world wasnae ye
  ah fed ye fire an fear
   beast giv ye
  craft tae warlock wi, boon ta mek
song iv deed an stone
  for a beast ye kept awake, on the rim

aye an the wars when ye wiz dragon spit
  afore, when ears had enormous rooms
  an each bairn bore a castle tae hoard the flame

  AAAURAGHGH! Twas me spit ye buggers oot
me stars amang yer wisht me tongues in yer bellies
   belchin the dancefire iv dawns, ready…

  Gies me hollow harp
   ah'l twang yiz a glint off the gem
    me gob's gettin hot
   me tail's ower lang tae pass
noo yer al sae fat wi tearin doon moontins
   aye, stuffin the land wi yer taste for iron
    an rivers turned tae steerin wheels
   an odd acre a sky burned for toast
    an not a beast tae crack yer mind a skull
not even a nip Godzilla in a matchbox destruction derby
   stuck on the telly's milkless tit
 ah'l fart an Age for yer
  creak an ague
   aye, ah like me meat pasty in the grimace
   ah'l lick yiz a spark or two

Am comin oot hinny!
me hungor cannae portent the cave namore
                a seen the glint amang thoo
                    silver an gold mongers plannin the debacle
survival only lasts a second anyroad's end

GASP! Am burnin for a feed
        am flyin in ye
yer ribs is the Himalayan Moontins
    an yer hearts a drum wi ancient rivers
        aye, am amang you lot
    am bangin on yer bones wi me empty plate

an afore ah scoff the lot
    ah'll kiss yer bonnie bright eyes luv
        aye, life alone is pure bonnie lass
                pure wi imprities whimper an all
        me flame is a reckonin
                    am a slither-monger for the moon's eye
                    open yersel an moan

aye am a local dragon
        lords an ladies of the knockin shop
            am loanin mesel oot for coffee an hot-tubs
        bring yer kids ah'l gollop them anall
            us dragonsingers are fussy
                we divn't like tae nibble

are ye settled?
        de ye have a bone for the nights?
            aright
me mithor was King an Queen iv the Sun

a real nabob
        she buggured the planet an like or bloody not
                am heor
        a flame from the cosmic gasworks
                come tae burn yer ass
            come tae mind thunder an corrupt horses

(ah'v eaten many a good horse
        an frogs iz nowt tae a famishin bloody dragon
                na more is a fat operatic cow
        tippin boss off ootside byredoor of a night
when me tiptoe wears oot an a trip ower tongue
                just aboot nigh on a smashin meat porker,
aye)

ah whisper lore tae horses through thin air
        an tickle the Polish underground
            wi the mention iv me flight
        it's dragon sex
    am daft aboot fire
        an me sister is Wata
            am liable tae pop up anyplace an clatter
                    ah'l crap in the holy grail
                bloody Druid cast that cup
        am nout but a smokin reptile on the beer

the hotblooded undergroond for elephants
        ah'v kept secret sperm count of rhinoceris
            in me knackers
for the war against IBM
(Bugger yer ma, you computerized etherized dots!)

am extinct as bad breath
　　　　when ah spit ye buggers oot
　　　　wipin me off
me, wi flamin throat an armor gaited soul
　　a flame a yard longer than reason
　　　　　　ah'l eat technology wi snot
　　ah'l clog the works wi dragon spit gannor smash

aye, comin doon road wi greenarsed measure
me eyes pokin through sky curtain
　　　dinnae stare
　　　　　　ye'll fall in
　　　　　　　it's deep
　　　　　　　aye the bloody dragondance it's lang
　　lang enough tae put yer arse asleep.

CANNY OLD DRUM

It's truth, aye truth aal dancing sings
summoning spins and spins
wi warlock arms o' spiral light
te call the dead from theor delight.

Aal things we love that nivor die
we sing them yem wi every sigh
muse-struck, roselip'd, luv shares
joy's weightless mystery of airs.

Knotted grander than oor parts
ships nor seasons, human hearts
wiser, don't dance, can't shift alone
awakened te centuries of bone.

Aye many ways there are te die!
As curtains close, human eye
shutters off each rising Sun
or seals its light from anyone.

Come bonnie lips, along me neck
ancient whispers of each step
as oor latest angel sings
how life unfolds its penny wings.

And noo, a candle, fragile host
in case, ower hurried of its ghost
we lose love's mystery an kiss
of fear that time must still exist.

PIT PONIES
(Seghill, 1949)

As a làd

    aah fed pit ponies in the dark;

blind, munchin miner's baccy as a treat

they'd take smaal bows an count theor feet.

Aah see each piebald eye, theor marbled world

made milky mad to wound the ground.

Alone, at work inside luv's cave

aah see a bonnie horse who gave and gave

and wake, afraid for hauling heavy coal

so deep inside me mithor earth, I'll die

and nivor live te kick the sky.

WICCAE

A lang time ago

        men in black
        dragged our wyrd lasses oot
an threw them on a fire.

They lay hewn timbers on the fire too
      aye, even used Jesus' cross
  for flames.

Ye can still see the ashes

      floating doon the gutters
      littering mountain trails
wounding the clearest streams.

DRĀGOMAN (poet-translator)

Aye, aa'm a drāgomon
gone wi lineage
daft,
      in the know, wyrd wi tongues.
    Ye whe can hear, know
        it's me time noo.
Aye...
Tek your time
    bonnie lamb
      lay a hand on dream
        reckon
    what's deep doon
        give it heart.
Ye might have anithor rememberin...sithee?
    Listen aal along your road.
        Listen on...
          aa'm a drāgomon
  ears
  not wings,
aa sing the salt road
      the way ower an back:
    come by me noo
    come by me noo...by...me...noo.
Don't be listenin te the Giant, why aye
    die asleep an
      everything te loathe
        gets fat!
      Tek yer time, bonnie lamb.

V.

CROUCHING OVER
THE KILL

(1984 - 1994)

· 🌿 ·

I have been the whale's body fifty-one years

and told no-one.

MERLIN'S TASK
IN THE CITY OF ANGELS
for Thomas Rain Crowe

It is at night slain as I am by darkness
when the shapeshifting moon rouses Druid dreams
to share their fugitive life from the sun, that sleepers
who lack details of vision to craft desire, fear most
the babbling longfingered hairy man with diamond eyes
who comes asking for water.
Still, a moon continues arousing oceans and inner life
sifting bloodtides, sorting revelations,
hunting songs and ancient stairs
inviting elusive kachinas to guide us to another country.
Too few are coming.
Infantile, hungry, ghosts of the masculine-feminine's
divided energy, recruit shadow armies
a manyheaded mass seduces children to become
instantly old; alien, scripted, unearthly
though born shining, naked as the familiarity of acorns.
Dawn, along the western rim a moon melts
seeking refuge in an oak tree, feathers heavy with oil.
How does a raven cross slippery rocks
and return to speak the language of birds?

ACCOUTREMENTS

Magic is its own reward

Just as the dancer

knows a motion in a sphere

invisibly within

Yet how it leaps without

to an audience

who, tongue-tied

secretly wave their thousand arms

and waft richly

toward and beyond death.

Just so, I say

do we drift in our soul—

Seasons and migrations

swirling through us

and no man to own this world

but its savouring!

ODIN

She takes off her dress and
spreads it on a chair,
dress of the thousand butterflies
he cannot touch.

For having lost the summer breath
of the Year King,
he only knows a road between the window and the door.

THE MAN WHO SAW GOD

I haven't seen God,
I have seen a man, a man who saw God.

He came over a dune with a tree on his back,
a shadow he stole from the sea,

his eyes—like nails.

Only the stars remain
    to show how his knees are broken,
    and have become glass.

DOOR BANGING IN THE HOUSE

A son calls for his father in the night.
He wants to learn how it feels
to be completely alive.

The father tells him to shape his own world:
"there are winners and losers, bigshots
and nobodies," the father's fist turns white,
his voice becomes the snake coiled in his son's belly.

From that moment, the boy can't touch ground.
Talking with other men
a hole in his chest yawns like a coyote's jaw,
a coyote with yellowglass eyes.

He tries to fill this wound with whiskey, women, money,
work, food, television, politics, art,
religion, cars, nuclear physics and other heavy drugs,
but there is never time to reach his father's
strangeness again.

One day, working alone in the woods, he cuts off
his father's head, chops off all the limbs
neatly at the trunk.

Stacking the logs under his house, the son begins
to weep, he weeps for a year, and
one night awakens and sees his sleeping wife's face.

He knows it is Spring and soon he will have white hair.

SUSAN SUNTREE'S BELLY

She has discovered the center of Earth.
It is so full of stars
the moon has to come out all the time.

Inside her, something is happening.
Schools of fish who chase my thoughts
have deserted me,
eyes lost by schoolteachers in the rain
look sideways at our belly and blink.

Perhaps, somehow, I am involved.
Possibly another mystery has appeared,
thinking of its name.
I am already fishing in the mountains:

if it is a boy we catch trout
if it is a girl we catch trout.

Now I remember, soon the year will grow a backache,
words will become more expensive,
a horse we do not own
will appear at the fence demanding hay.

We will feed it and live at the center of Earth
caressing its blue limits with a small hand.

HOME BIRTH
for Califia

My lips trembled, I was still immigrating West
    at sixty miles per hour.
Face to face with birth, a newborn
    dipped in blue whey with eyes like Earth.
Eyes still searching among the planets for milk,

I lifted her from the womb, that infinity hole,
    catching the aroma of the deep veldt
hearing from the cave the old chants,
    bent again like a bushman to the new kill,
sensing at my back the roar and teeth, hunched again
    'round the new wriggling one, lips, sweet budlips,
grubfists tucked in the bignight tumbling.

Then I gave her to the breasts and was a man again,
    wolfeye'd one, streetsloucher,
stuffing stars in my pockets, the hairy man
  among the thornbushes watching mother and child
    retreat into their world like clouds back through a canyon.

Mammal blood dried on my hands, maps there among hills
    and another solitude to the music of sucking.

I am a "new man" but my womb is the same serape around the fire.
    When I hesitate to plunge a knife in the bear's belly
    my woman's eyes glitter like moonlit water.
I throw wood on a fire like Jesse James counting the cash.

ELEUSIS

Thinking I know nothing
about the great nothing
        is like kissing
    the woman I thought too beautiful
        for myself
    and feeling hello and goodbye
        on my own lips.
When I am a life raft
drifting alone on the Pacific
    learning to love the sea
        and a storm comes, I know
    I am singing to my own death.
        I discover a hand on the wood
    of a tree sliced into a desk
is a view of great plains
        where darker files of animals
    bow their heads as the sun sets
        feeling
    the prayer of a journey
for the heart of this Earth
    and a chorus of return
        when men wave white flowers,
    fields are white flowers,
        the sky is white flowers,
    white flowers.

AFTER SAIGON

for Glen

Among monuments where flowers wilt
I reckon death as air
remembering how mothers bleed sweet milk
to fuse the day and night.

I am no more America's child
who dies to sleep
beneath these quilted States forever young.

Born life's servant with bright eyes
I now know war from beauty.
Friends help me seek mortality
among all these hungry ghosts.

A POLISH RESTAURANT
IN CALIFORNIA

By now I have been gliding for years
between dim candles
and the conversational elegance of bread
to wait upon the mountain in every human face;
becoming "American."

I have poured myself in eyes,
seen gods within
cease caring if our sacred intimacy survives.

I want a pale horse on the hill to appear
riderless forever,
warriors to remain waiters
serving this Earth in our silent black shoes.

TROUBLE

Once I fucked God's wife.
God was away at a spiritual retreat.

Our affair began simply. I was sitting around a campfire
and this woman caressed my behind.

How was she to know I'm such an easy lay?
How was I to know she was God's wife?

She *felt* a lot like somebody else's wife,
especially when she talked about God.

But as they say: "a rising penis has no conscience";
until God came home.

By now, I knew quite a lot about God.
He's been angry for a long time.

He called me. My feet were cold as hairy mammoths
but I went. The man wept, threatening
to break my arms, and he was as big as God.

I listened. His wife cried. I swore not to
fool around with the wife.

From now on, whenever God calls, I'm not going.

IN ZEUS'S BIRTHPLACE
(Crete, 1987)

Existing at some distance from the light
      I kept my eyes shielded from the gods.
   They guided me into walls
       courthouse walls, cell walls, bus station walls,
          motel walls with their parchment night.
I ran from solitude with the usual lies.
      My charming masks attracted lovers
                to themselves.
I am not proud of the dust on my tongue,
      some memories are the same as attempting
           to introduce visitors
    to the ghost of an accident.
My lips, softened by a gentler truth,
      thirst to touch whatever
         makes flesh translucent.
After Zeus's cave I kept the echoes of my own breath
      down there, in the cave.
    The cave is uterine, fissured, womb-walled.
    There is nowhere deeper than these eyes.

THE TUMBLING

Laundry piles up with things unsaid,
to be washed after dark,
spun dry and folded in dreams of whole cloth
torn, because I am tumbling in lives
of two children, two marriages
and my wife won medals in high school debate.

Round and round behind lensed glass
tumbles our union of love and hate.
Ghostflap of arms and legs.
Life and death's braid of knots.
Death and love's tumultuous horses
mounting and remounting in fate's wild gypsy wedding.

I have heard stories of teenagers
joyriding in gas dryers
who died tumbling in pairs,
entangled, suffocated
by desire for another emerging life
to spring from these mounds of dirty laundry.

Buddha, I am not detachment's lover yet
and do I want a partner, too,
with anima and animus balanced
as a Heisman trophy winner in drag
whose masculine and feminine aspects
leap however sexual police snap their fingers—
a person who washes dishes, mops floors,
chops wood, milks the kid, fixes the car,
attends men's groups, women's groups, drinks
androgynous juice and loosens the grip
of Zeus on his spear?

But I lost the housekey among credit cards
and liberating magazine poems
about men who despoil goddesses placed between
ads about how to make it to a Mercedes
and stay feminine in corporate suits
thin ties, thin cigarettes and thin values.
I have locked myself out
and will climb through the window again
when this mountain of laundry is done.

FINDING THE SUN

All the Sun does is shine.
Even in the deepest cloud
the Sun shines.

I sat on my father's deathbed
and listened to him say:
"Son, your teeth are so white."

If I laugh in these mirrors
my friends will all know
and the revenge of my enemies
will lose its map.

When there is light in my heart
I know what lives forever:
all these life forms
leaping from star to star,
and my body, a small adobe motel,
visited by the laughter of secret lovers.

FOR MY FATHER,
DEAD OF LEUKEMIA

The great redwoods logged years ago

none left to rise above the second growth

reaching for sky on spindly legs

and people, measuring trees against their old cuts.

Stumps are why sons love mothers

more than they know men

and in small rooms we argue into the night.

ON JOHN DONNE'S COFFIN

I must have come to Los Angeles to watch television.
All day I lie on the couch and stare
watching detective stories about men without souls.
When they catch one, they kill another,
and then I am educated about cars, deodorant and soap.

Later, in the evening, childish husbands obey impatient wives,
adolescents reach maturity before seven o'clock
and everything works out fine.

Because my mother and father were addicted,
I chose to watch this horror another forty years
from the hole in the livingroom
where fear devoured love.

I don't care about people who don't
smoke cigarettes or eat red meat.
I have been tasting the dragon's breath
as it winds through a nightmare of centuries.

My soul lifts slowly off the couch onto channel five
and whales beach themselves on the sand.
If I have completed anything in my life it is this sleep.

CROUCHING OVER THE KILL

I see you stone mother, among this weather of dreams
    where wars men made, made you deaf to my screams.

The cradle I rock is mine, mine all alone
    with its rockers of time and blankets of bone.

Among lovers like cellos in midsummer dust
    I have sashayed for angels with elephant lust.

I'd wear any mask for a sweet mother's eyes, father
    any erection in any disguise.

I've hunted your darkness, married our nights, youth's
    milky abyss of dreadful delights.

Now Pan's penny wings don't pulse in my bed.
    I'll seek a wise woman for kinship instead.

ECOLOGY

In a small town called Anywhere,
semis hurtle down the highway.
A streetlight is hurled on the ground.

A doe wanders across a parking lot
nosing into smelly dumpsters
and storefront doorways,
her watery shadow across the blacktop.

In the morning the town awakens.
The deer has gone.
No one knows she was there.
Even the sleepy security guard
who watched her all night long.

BECAUSE GOLD SLIPS
FROM OUR FINGERS

A cab takes bride and groom to the Instant Hotel
where two broken sticks make a fire,

only children remain to watch the flames.

WHAT THE LAST CRICKET SAID

Listen. There are five ways
out of this city:
north, south, east, west
and the graveyard.

SOMALIA

Past the forty days of temptation.
Past the forty days of solitude.
Past the scriptures of bread and water,
she travels further than prayer
down death's bony human river
in shrunken weather that does not change,
weather she has seen before.
She sees the hunchbacked hyena lope.
She sees the Sun turn fat.
She sees there is night, sees there is day
mute as her long march past hell
past heaven, past advice of saints
whose compassion is wind, dry wind.
The cracked lava soles of her feet.
The vulture bones of her ankles.
Her eyes deeper than Zeus's cave.
Sockets scooped by a lion's paw,
scooped by Somalia's dunecarving scalpel,
a shadow there, an iris there,
the infinity there where she sees
sand and rocks, sand and rocks without God.
Sees. Sees how a woman lies down.
Lies down in our dance, turning.
Lies down, lies down
whirling, roaring. The spinning there
where the Universe retreats black, from its stars.
There where I am going. There where she is gone.

FORTUNE MAGAZINE
MEETS JESSE JAMES

The cash

banks keep handy today

wouldn't buy a good hat.

Banks have television surveillance

and there's no country left to ride

and too damn little cash.

What I'd really like to do

is hogtie the five hundred richest sonsbitches

in the USA to an honest job

and pay 'em minimum wage

as an act of violence no different

than the carpetbagger scum who created

an enduring kinship between folk and Jesse James.

FRANK & JESSE

I want to rob banks again.

To take

the certainty from men in suits

whose boundaries

stop at a blade of grass

because their old world

needs cash to contain the soul.

I have no guns

and in a heartbeat I too

am dead, but birds

are my friends and the eyes of the poor

burn fierce as the Sun.

NEWS FROM THE BALKANS

side Sarajevo it was snowing, the dead
e stiffly from their graves
d looked around.
oden crosses cast a human shadow.
sted trees cast a human shadow.
olitary crow cast a human shadow.
new turned earth lay a human shadow.
man shadow! Human shadow!
now, the dead knew: men become what they hate.
t their voice had been given to war.
eir eyes were haunted.
eir ribs were a city of ruined temples
ere they had not listened.
one had listened to the dead.
e dead who speak so gently, the dead who say:
O OLD GODS ARE FIGHTING OVER ONE CRUST OF BREAD
men became bullets, broken wagonwheels,
stroyed children and shelled oatfields.
ey became wounds that zigzag
m East to West, from North to South.
unds like comicbook scars from Transylvania
rn by vampires in army uniforms
o play soccer between artillery engagements.
n became the weary history of heroism and boredom
ause the cold war had been so cold.
TIL EVERY MAN IS A DOVE THE WAY IS DARK...say the dead,
dead who die alone and make their way, over the frosty hills,
o houses and trenches, into prisoncamps and wretched hospitals,
o surplus gasoline cans and canteens, and into air.
o the air that Earth breathes. Into Earth's blood. Into
rth's emerging Balkanized culture of blood.

LAST ANGELS

Earth's vanishing angels are singing again.
Where they reside, between the wind of an elephant's ear
and the lips of a dreaming child.
I have seen men wave arms at their women,
shouting down sirens in gossamer dresses
who were burned in Ghent five hundred years ago.
But the angels keep singing
even as they fly deep into cellular reality
to hibernate like white bears
melting with polar ice, melting of the heat
still radiating from catholic fires
lit by men who no longer believed in wings.
I hear the angels singing in the prairie grass
that rustler's song that rides for love,
whispering in purple and yellow and red
to seeds, crouched foetuses, to camouflaged fawns,
how human skin has become the Wells Fargo safe
impenetrable to less than dynamite
no longer disturbed by the caress of an angel's song.

THIS AGE CLEARCUTS
ITS HEARTWOOD

This Age clearcuts its heartwood,
makes duff of Earth's sweet offering.

Ragged, omen harsh, a scavenger,
I haunt backroads with topaz eyes
unseen by hasty humans who fear their own death.

On crags, seacliffs or here,
sidestepping Calafia's forked limbs
high where flickers, jays and mapgies chat, I hunch.

As for lovers who spurn tomorrow, dawnlight on feathers
will transform ebony to a ruby flash
for each sense is tested by their vanishing.

THE CHERUBIM

for my students

I too am concerned about scientists measuring air.
Lawyers in chariots depositing oxygen in the bank.
Unwanted conversations dissolving in French hormone pills
and large sea mammals coming ashore to watch.

I make my morning vigil over eggs
smiling at this breakfast with Miro.
All of my work is inside these ordinary eggs.

I have walked to school for twenty years.
A family clings to my body.
I go to suckle a dewy host that sips from unseen flowers.

THINGS MEN DO ALONE

Where is the drum music coming from?
The Horn of Africa is full of puppets.
Fire is being drained from the sand.
The camel marts are crowded with tanks.

Here come the castanets. Chattering teeth
to awaken the dancer.
Death takes a rose between her lips
and walks me across the floor.

In a silver mirror of my own silence, I dance.
My pelvic eyes flashing darkness and light.
Under my feet the Earth
is slowly turning for a new moon's smile.

I close the curtains. Soon enough
this busy Age comes plundering
to seek an ordinary body for its crowded disembodied self.

ECLIPSE

for Albert Lightning

The moon eclipses in November
a gift: to be shadowless on Earth
listening to bones
as the sea sound of a seashell
seems the shore of life exhaling.
I surrender to exhalations
this winter breath.
So many tongues in tongues,
the hordes invading verbs
shades in this shade
so I with no further obligations
trace this frail americano track
across the California dark
lingering as a child plays
in soot
to scratch my own graffiti.
     There are green angels
on tossed seas
pirates for the soul of whales
and reasoned men at home
with time on their wrists.
My children
have never drawn a clean breath
like vast shoals of various fish
they drift in lugubrious schools.
History is a gill net.
     Crazy Horse
waved his lance
at the boys in blue
looked into bodies
declaring victory
at what eventuality he saw.
He saw fools.
    "Leave everything a spot cleaner

for your passin," my mother said,
(she smoked herself to death).
I seek ecology, wage kinship
wrestling for roots, locked
sensualities of temple gods,
the mature masculine.
It feels no longer fierce to be seized
by a life contained
by civilized indignity.
I will tattoo my face, use Zeus's
simplest prerogatives, plant seeds
and see them through.
I want to know hunting
as the stranger finding a tree in the woods
recognized himself.
I want to dare a barefoot precipice
reckon contemporary insanity
against ancient madness.
                    After slipped horizons,
on a lover's breast
I want to whisper Teton winds
                    engorge arteries
antlers,
that pulse, our coming.
                    Is this restlessness
old or young?

                    I have the compassionless face of ancestors
who hewed coal, followed a plow
at home in harness,
my stumbling feather fetlock hoofprints
my fancy dance. Along the matrix fields
I haul my poet's plow
scattering seed: *pomegranate,*
thighbone, fibula, conch shell, sagebrush,
hoof, watercress, water table, amoeba,
buffalo chips, prairie grass, chipmunk
rib, madrone, grandfather, mouse, dragonfly.........

I have dived in an infant's newborn eyes
and soul to soul, bypassed rational connections
to "communication."
      I need not take a shovel
to the Gobi desert
to excavate a miraculousness
whose bones are in our face!
I have seen bushmen hoard batteries
in gourds etched with Giraffes.
In Los Angeles' museums
Egyptian mummies
wreathed in gold
listen disinterred, to pop music
carried by High School students
who never heard of the Nile.
Does time exist?

        My family embraces trees
plants corn
identifies garden "pests" by name.
I keep acorns for a passport.
I have seen humans
in antiseptic corridors
run from natural birth
and pass out cigars,
witnessed lifetimes spent
dusting mantlepieces.
I have been prisoner of untouched dreams
awakened behind real bars
heard my father's violent hand
become a cell's slow hinge,
paid rent meekly
while mailmen terrorized
by imagined social necessity
stuffed marriages with advertisements
for oil changes, carpet cleanings, life insurance.
(They won! They won!)

I am the frozen sperm of progress,
a despotism.
For me, the "second coming"
is of a clean sea.
I live and die in a bardo cataract
of a hundred million life-forms
lightning visitor to Earth.
My affection for the travail of each person
is monitored by the Sun.
          I found my bones on shores
of a subarctic lake
watching geese,
slapping blackflies
a perspective
hillocked by wildflowers
toothless caribou herders
squinting into bottles of *Koskinkourva*.
Mosquitoes chased me
from the Paleolithic.

       (I am slouching to the movies
to be born.)

No cynic,
I hasten history's hoarded ferocity.
I believe jazz and bagpipes
offer the same ancestral
lyricism. I accept
romantics as infants
who neglect details
in favor of imagined universal instants
and then it rains.
I accept first original gasps
after natural grief
as true song.
I have heard wolves
make rounder music
than the Renaissance.

I believe dolphins
optimize mermaid consciousness
solving the fossil fuel problem
over three-fifths of Earth.
On a species level, technocratic humans
are God's parasitic mold
slowly inhaling
anti-existential gas.
                    Because courage is a capable solitude
there is a sky.
Because I can hear
myriad burdenbearers
laboring
in a beeswarm
I know the Grand Canyon
maps native inner life.
I have lived to see
the Industrial Revolution
become an anarchy of bloodtypes.
I have seen the war against patriarchy
become a haircut.

I have lived to see
American spacewalks become
less challenging than coming home late.
I am witnessing childhood
become an experience
reserved for adults.
There is gunfire in my alley.
Children in my city
who think milk comes from bottles
and chickens have no feathers.
I have listened to arctic lake ice
form near Rovaniemi
a sheet at a time, whispering, frozen layers,
hurled instantly
magically to veil water
realizing

comprehension of phenomena
has been abandoned by man
for his own image.
I have been wyrdly drawn by reindeer
to wander ceaselessly
experiencing
how mammals loft antlers in psyche's
pulsing underwear.
Cities, clans, will be feudal again
migrant tides gather again,
planetary tides:
...Brazil's favella danceocracy...
Mexico's feudal mafiocracy...
Russia's desperado garage sale...
Poland's street-theatre...
England's polite assassinations...
France's eternal milk strike...
Germany's platonic gearshifts...
Canada's provincial solitaire...
China's great unelected thumb...
India's sacred wrestling match...
Africa's diamond guillotine...
Japan's deferential glutamates...
America's monocultured franchise...
undone, undone
undone by air
undone by earth
undone by water
undone by fire.
An ancient ceremonial decay.

The eclipse is done.
I see my shadow on the floor
and now for bed
where gods set sails for dreams:
To wake with mountains
in the soul,
and then the sun
that licks my ribs
with its own quick dragon's tongue.

THE CANADA GEESE

for Salley

Let us not make too much sense

especially of desire

or we will never travel

like the hummingbird

found under a migrating goose's wing.

So many departures

like the hands

of waving children

assure me, mortality

will soon be over.

Like water, you also

pass through centuries

with me and without me.

In winter, when the mountain

proves what is not important

we fall in snow

until spring awakens and we are gone.

HIGHER IN THE MOUNTAINS

(Taos, N.M.)

From here, I can see a long way
to the western sea
where along its shaky crack
people are building more walls.
Sometimes, in the afternoon
when the big clouds roll in
a shadow launches itself
from a ledge
in the reefs of thunder
descending in the predatory drop
of a bird whose dilated gaze
has seen the gods,
and I stand
in salutory joyousness, ready
to meet the eagle eye to eye.

AUTHOR'S BIOGRAPHY

Philip James Daughtry was born a fraternal twin, near Newcastle upon Tyne, England, in 1942. His mother and his mother's father were sergeants in the British Army. On his father's side, he is related to legendary "Old West" American outlaws Frank and Jesse James. He migrated to Canada in 1957 then to the United States. After two years at the University of Denver, he dropped out to cowboy his way further West. He received an MFA from U.C. Irvine in 1971 and has since alternatively worked various jobs, taught and travelled in Finland, Brazil, England, and Central America. In addition to completing three screenplays, his work has appeared in such journals and anthologies as *City Lights Review, Co-Evolution Quarterly, NEW Canadian & American Poetry, Western Poetry Review, Whole Earth Catalog, Blind Donkey,* and *Coyote's Journal.* His previous books are *The Stray Moon* and *Kid Nigredo.* Currently he lives in Santa Monica, California, where he is a guest lecturer in Filmic Writing at the Lucas Film School, a story development consultant for the Canadian Film Board and a professor of English & Environmental Studies at Santa Monica College.

Limited Cloth Edition
May 1995
#22 of 25
Philip Daughtry